THE DIGITAL MIND

How Computers Mimic Human Thinking.

Golf Ofuka

gcodecloud GmbH

Copyright © 24.12.2024 gcodecloud GmbH

All rights reserved

The characters and events portrayed in this book are NON-fictitious. Any similarity to real persons, living or dead, is coincidental and not intended by the author.

No part of this book may be reproduced, or stored in a retrieval system, or transmitted in any form or by any means, electronic, mechanical, photocopying, recording, or otherwise, without express written permission of the publisher.

ISBN-13: 9798304738330
ISBN-10: 9798304738330

Cover design by: gcodecloud GmbH
Printed in the United States of America

Dedication

To The Lord and my family—your unwavering love, support, and belief in me have been the foundation of my resilience and success.

To my team at gcodecloud GmbH and Mega Phonebook Nig—this is for your dedication, passion, and commitment to turning vision into reality.

To every tech leader, entrepreneur, and dreamer navigating innovation challenges—may this book inspire you to lead with courage, resilience, and purpose.

This is for those who dare to build, to lead, and to transform the future.

CONTENTS

Title Page
Copyright
Dedication
Introduction
Chapter 1   1
Chapter 2   6
Chapter 3   13
Chapter 4   19
Chapter 5   25
Chapter 6   31
Chapter 7   38
Chapter 8   45
Chapter 9   51
Chapter 10   58
About The Author   65

INTRODUCTION

The question of whether machines can think has fascinated humanity for decades, sparking debate among scientists, philosophers, and engineers alike. Today, in the age of artificial intelligence, the line between human thought and machine processes is no longer just a theoretical discussion—it's a reality shaping our world.

From virtual assistants that understand natural language to algorithms capable of diagnosing diseases and driving cars, computers are performing tasks that were once considered the sole domain of human intelligence. But how do they do it? How can systems built from silicon chips and lines of code replicate the intricacies of human cognition?

The Digital Mind: How Computers Mimic Human Thinking dives deep into these questions, unraveling the mechanisms behind intelligent machines and the ways they emulate human thought processes. This book is your guide to understanding how the digital systems we rely on daily are designed to perceive, learn, and make decisions.

The Journey from Brain to Machine

At the heart of this exploration lies the connection between the human brain and computational models. While our brains function through a network of neurons transmitting electrical signals, computers process information through algorithms and circuits. The parallels are striking, yet the differences are just as profound. This book delves into how engineers and researchers have drawn inspiration from neuroscience to create machines capable of pattern recognition, reasoning, and even creativity.

Why This Book Matters

Understanding how computers mimic human thinking is not just a technical curiosity—it's essential knowledge for navigating the modern world. As artificial intelligence becomes more pervasive, its influence touches every aspect of life, from healthcare and education to business and entertainment. Whether you're a tech professional, a business leader, or simply a curious mind, grasping the fundamentals of how machines think empowers you to engage critically with these technologies and their implications.

What You'll Discover

Throughout this book, you'll explore:

- The foundational principles of machine intelligence and how they parallel human cognition.
- The evolution of AI technologies, from simple algorithms to advanced neural networks.
- Real-world applications of intelligent systems in industries like healthcare, transportation, and commerce.
- The ethical and societal challenges posed by machines that mimic human thought.

A Personal Connection

My fascination with the intersection of human cognition and machine intelligence began with a simple question: How does a machine solve problems like a person does? Over the years, I've had the privilege of witnessing groundbreaking advancements in AI and computational science, which have inspired me to share this journey with you. This book is not just about the technology—it's about understanding how it shapes the world around us and our role within it.

Join me as we explore the digital mind, unravel its mysteries, and discover how the machines of today are redefining what it means to think. Together, we'll uncover how artificial intelligence isn't just about mimicking human thought—it's about expanding what's possible in the world of tomorrow.

Welcome to *The Digital Mind: How Computers Mimic Human Thinking*. Let's begin.

CHAPTER 1

INTRODUCTION TO THE DIGITAL MIND

The Intersection of Technology and Human Cognition

The intersection of technology and human cognition represents a pivotal area of exploration in understanding how computers can emulate human thought processes. This relationship has evolved significantly with advances in artificial intelligence, machine learning, and cognitive computing. By examining how technology can mimic and enhance human cognitive capabilities, students and tech founders can gain insights into the potential applications and implications of these technologies in various fields.

At the core of this intersection is the concept of neural networks, which are inspired by the structure and function of the human brain. These computational models consist of interconnected nodes that process information in a manner reminiscent of neuronal connections. By training these networks on vast datasets, machines can learn to recognize patterns, make predictions, and even generate creative outputs, simulating aspects of human thought. Understanding the principles behind neural networks is essential for computer students, as it lays the groundwork for developing more sophisticated algorithms that can tackle complex problems.

Cognitive computing takes this a step further by incorporating elements of human reasoning, learning, and adaptation into technology. Systems designed with cognitive capabilities can analyze unstructured data, understand natural language, and engage in dialogue, offering a more human-like interaction with users. For tech founders, harnessing cognitive computing can lead to the creation of innovative products that provide personalized experiences, enhance decision-making processes, and improve user engagement. This represents a significant shift in how technology can augment human abilities rather than merely automate tasks.

Moreover, the ethical implications of blending technology with human cognition cannot be overlooked. As machines become more adept at mimicking human thought, questions arise regarding the potential consequences for privacy, autonomy, and employment. It is crucial for computer students and tech founders to engage with these ethical considerations to ensure that the technologies they create serve to empower individuals and society rather than diminish human agency. Developing frameworks for responsible AI and promoting transparency in algorithms are essential steps towards navigating these challenges.

Finally, the future of this intersection holds exciting possibilities. As research continues to advance, the potential for creating systems that not only replicate but also enhance human cognition is on the horizon. Whether it involves augmenting memory, improving problem-solving skills, or even fostering emotional intelligence in machines, the implications for education, healthcare, and various industries are profound. By understanding the synergy between technology and human cognition, students and founders can position themselves at the forefront of innovation, driving the next wave of advancements that redefine the boundaries of both fields.

Importance of Understanding Computer Mimicry

The concept of computer mimicry serves as a cornerstone for understanding how machines can replicate human cognitive processes. By examining the ways in which computers imitate human thought, students and tech founders can appreciate the intricacies involved in both the design and functionality of artificial intelligence systems. This understanding is crucial, as it not only informs the development of smarter algorithms but also shapes the ethical considerations surrounding their use. A foundational grasp of computer mimicry equips individuals in the tech industry with the insights needed to innovate responsibly.

One of the primary reasons to delve into the study of computer mimicry is the profound impact it has on the development of intelligent systems. From neural networks that resemble the structure of the human brain to algorithms designed to simulate decision-making processes, understanding how these systems work is vital for future advancements. For computer students, this knowledge forms the bedrock of their technical education, fostering a deeper comprehension of how to build and refine technologies that can better serve human needs. For tech founders, this insight can lead to more effective business strategies that leverage artificial intelligence for competitive advantage.

Moreover, understanding computer mimicry offers insights into the limitations and challenges inherent in AI. While computers can emulate certain aspects of human thinking, they often fall short in areas such as emotional intelligence, creativity, and contextual understanding. By recognizing these limitations, computer students can approach their projects with a balanced perspective, striving to enhance technology while acknowledging its current boundaries. Tech founders, too, can benefit from this understanding as they navigate the complexities of market expectations and the capabilities of the technology they are developing.

Ethical considerations also play a significant role in the importance of understanding computer mimicry. As technology advances, the potential for misuse increases, making it imperative for those in the field to recognize the moral implications of their work. Knowledge of how computers mimic human cognition can guide ethical decision-making, ensuring that developers prioritize transparency, accountability, and fairness in their creations. This awareness is essential in fostering trust among users and stakeholders, which is particularly important in an era where technology is deeply integrated into daily life.

Finally, the study of computer mimicry enriches the dialogue between technology and society. As machines increasingly influence human behavior and decision-making, understanding the parallels and divergences between human thought and machine processing becomes crucial. For computer students, this knowledge encourages interdisciplinary collaboration, combining insights from psychology, neuroscience, and computer science. For tech founders, it opens avenues for innovation that not only push technological boundaries but also address societal needs and concerns. Emphasizing the importance of this understanding will ultimately lead to more holistic and responsible advancements in the field of artificial intelligence.

CHAPTER 2

THE HUMAN BRAIN: A COMPLEX SYSTEM

Structure and Function of Neurons

Neurons are the fundamental building blocks of the nervous system, responsible for transmitting information throughout the body. Structurally, a neuron consists of three main parts: the cell body, dendrites, and axon. The cell body contains the nucleus and organelles, serving as the metabolic center of the neuron. Dendrites are tree-like extensions that receive signals from other neurons, while the axon is a long, slender projection that transmits electrical impulses away from the cell body to other neurons, muscles, or glands. The intricate design of neurons allows for complex communication networks, which are crucial for both human cognition and for drawing parallels in computer architecture.

The function of neurons is primarily based on their ability to transmit electrical signals, known as action potentials. When a neuron receives a sufficient stimulus through its dendrites, it generates an action potential that travels down the axon. This process involves the movement of ions across the neuron's membrane, leading to a rapid change in electrical charge. The action potential is an all-or-nothing response, meaning that once the threshold is reached, the neuron fires completely. This characteristic is akin to binary signals in computer systems, where information is transmitted as distinct on-off states.

Neurons communicate with each other at specialized junctions called synapses. When an action potential reaches the axon terminals, it triggers the release of neurotransmitters, which are chemical messengers that cross the synaptic cleft to bind to receptors on the adjacent neuron's dendrites. This interaction can either excite or inhibit the receiving neuron, influencing its likelihood of firing an action potential. The complexity of synaptic connections allows for a vast array of information processing and storage, similar to how data is managed and exchanged within computer networks.

The role of myelin sheaths in neuronal function is also significant. Myelin, a fatty substance, insulates axons and allows for faster transmission of action potentials through a process known as saltatory conduction. This mechanism ensures that electrical signals can travel more efficiently across long distances within the nervous system. The presence of myelin is comparable to the insulation of electrical wires in computer systems, which reduces signal degradation and enhances overall performance.

Understanding the structure and function of neurons provides valuable insights into the design of artificial intelligence and machine learning systems. By mimicking the way neurons process and transmit information, computer scientists can develop algorithms that emulate human cognitive functions. This knowledge not only advances technology but also fosters interdisciplinary collaboration, bridging the gap between neuroscience and computer engineering. As we explore the digital mind, the parallels between biological and artificial systems become increasingly relevant, highlighting the potential for innovation in both fields.

Neural Networks and Their Significance

Neural networks are a subset of machine learning methodologies designed to simulate the way the human brain processes information. Inspired by the biological neural networks that constitute human cognition, these computational models consist of interconnected nodes or "neurons." Each neuron receives inputs, processes them, and transmits outputs to subsequent neurons. This architecture allows neural networks to learn from data, adapt to new information, and improve their performance over time. As the foundation of many artificial intelligence applications, neural networks have become vital in fields such as image recognition, natural language processing, and autonomous systems.

The significance of neural networks lies in their ability to model complex patterns and relationships within vast datasets. Traditional algorithms often struggle with problems involving non-linear relationships or high-dimensional spaces. In contrast, neural networks excel in these scenarios by leveraging multiple layers of interconnected neurons to capture intricate dependencies. This depth allows them to learn hierarchical representations of data, making them particularly effective for tasks such as detecting objects in images or interpreting the nuances of human language. The flexibility and power of neural networks have led to significant advancements in AI capabilities, enabling machines to perform tasks that were previously thought to require human intelligence.

Neural networks also facilitate the development of deep learning, a specialized area of machine learning that utilizes architectures with many layers, known as deep neural networks. These deep networks have demonstrated remarkable success in various applications, including speech recognition, game playing, and even medical diagnosis. By stacking layers of neurons, deep learning models can analyze and extract features at multiple levels of abstraction, leading to more accurate predictions and insights. The proliferation of large datasets and increased computational power has further propelled the growth of deep learning, allowing researchers and practitioners to tackle increasingly complex problems.

Moreover, the significance of neural networks extends beyond their technical capabilities; they also raise important philosophical and ethical questions. As machines become more adept at mimicking human cognitive functions, the implications of their decisions and actions warrant careful consideration.

Issues such as bias in training data, the opacity of model decision-making processes, and the potential impact on employment and privacy are critical areas of concern. For computer students and tech founders, understanding the societal ramifications of neural networks is essential for responsible innovation and the development of ethical AI systems.

In conclusion, neural networks represent a pivotal advancement in the field of artificial intelligence, bridging the gap between human cognitive processes and machine learning. Their capacity to learn from complex data, adapt to new challenges, and enhance decision-making capabilities underscores their transformative potential. As these technologies continue to evolve, it is imperative for those in the tech industry to remain informed about both their technical merits and ethical implications. By doing so, they can harness the power of neural networks to drive innovation while ensuring that the benefits of AI are realized in a responsible and equitable manner.

Cognitive Processes: Memory, Learning, and Decision Making

Cognitive processes are fundamental to understanding how both human minds and computers operate. Memory, learning, and decision-making are interrelated processes that influence how information is processed and utilized. In humans, memory serves as the repository of experiences and knowledge, allowing individuals to retrieve relevant information when needed. This capacity is crucial for learning, as it enables the assimilation of new information by connecting it with existing memories. In computers, memory functions similarly, albeit in a more structured and often deterministic manner, where data is stored, retrieved, and manipulated based on algorithms designed to mimic human cognitive functions.

Learning in humans can be viewed as the development of new

skills or the alteration of existing knowledge through experience. It occurs through various mechanisms, such as reinforcement learning, where positive outcomes reinforce specific behaviors, or observational learning, where individuals learn by observing others. In contrast, machine learning algorithms emulate this process by identifying patterns in data and improving their performance over time. By training on vast datasets, these algorithms can recognize complex patterns that may not be immediately apparent, thereby mimicking the human capacity for learning and adapting to new information.

Decision-making represents a critical cognitive function that relies on both memory and learning. Humans often make decisions based on a combination of past experiences, emotional responses, and rational analysis. This multifaceted approach allows individuals to weigh options and consider potential outcomes effectively. In the realm of computing, decision-making processes are often modeled after these human strategies. Algorithms such as decision trees and neural networks are employed to analyze data and make predictions or recommendations, reflecting the ways humans process information to arrive at conclusions.

The interplay between memory, learning, and decision-making highlights the importance of cognitive architectures in artificial intelligence. These architectures aim to replicate human-like thinking patterns by integrating various cognitive processes into a cohesive system. For instance, a cognitive architecture might utilize a combination of short-term and long-term memory storage to inform decision-making processes, similar to how humans retrieve relevant information to guide their choices. This approach not only enhances the efficiency of computational models but also brings them closer to replicating human cognitive functions.

As technology advances, understanding these cognitive processes becomes increasingly vital for computer students and tech founders. By grasping how memory, learning, and decision-making operate within both humans and machines, they can design more intuitive and effective AI systems. This knowledge enables the creation of technologies that not only perform tasks efficiently but also adapt and evolve, much like the human mind. The ongoing exploration of cognitive processes will undoubtedly shape the future of AI, leading to innovations that bridge the gap between human thought and digital intelligence.

CHAPTER 3

FOUNDATIONS OF COMPUTER SCIENCE

Overview of Computer Architecture

Computer architecture refers to the conceptual design and fundamental operational structure of a computer system. It encompasses the physical components of a computer, such as the central processing unit (CPU), memory, and input/output devices, as well as the functional organization of these components. Understanding computer architecture is essential for computer students and tech founders, as it provides the foundational knowledge necessary for designing and developing efficient computing systems. The architecture of a computer can significantly influence its performance, capability, and compatibility with various applications, including those that aim to mimic human cognitive processes.

At the core of computer architecture is the CPU, often referred to as the brain of the computer. The CPU is responsible for executing instructions from programs, performing calculations, and managing data flow within the system. It consists of several key components, including the arithmetic logic unit (ALU), which performs mathematical operations, and the control unit (CU), which directs the operation of the processor by coordinating the activities of the other components. The design of the CPU can greatly affect how well a computer can perform tasks that require complex computations or rapid processing, similar to the functions of the human brain.

Memory architecture is another critical aspect of computer architecture. It involves the organization and management of various types of memory, including primary memory (RAM), secondary storage (hard drives, SSDs), and cache memory. The speed and efficiency of data retrieval and storage are vital for optimal performance, particularly in applications that process large volumes of information or require real-time responses. Understanding how different memory types work together can provide insights into how computers can achieve tasks analogous to human memory, such as storing and recalling information.

Input and output (I/O) systems are also integral to computer architecture. They facilitate communication between the computer and the external environment, allowing users to interact with the system and receive output. I/O devices include keyboards, mice, printers, and displays, among others. The design of I/O systems influences the user experience and the overall functionality of the computer. By exploring how I/O systems operate, tech founders can better appreciate the importance of creating intuitive interfaces that enhance user interaction, much like the sensory inputs and outputs that humans experience.

Finally, the evolution of computer architecture has been driven by advances in technology and the growing demands of complex applications. Innovations such as parallel processing, multicore processors, and cloud computing have transformed traditional architectures, enabling computers to perform tasks previously thought to be exclusive to human cognition. As computer students and tech founders delve deeper into the intricacies of computer architecture, they will gain valuable insights into how these systems can be optimized to better mimic human thought processes, paving the way for future developments in artificial intelligence and machine learning.

Algorithms and Their Role in Problem Solving

Algorithms serve as the backbone of problem-solving in computational contexts, drawing parallels between the structured methods used by the human brain to tackle complex tasks. At their core, algorithms are step-by-step procedures that provide a systematic approach to solving a problem or performing a computation. Just as humans engage in logical reasoning and employ heuristics to navigate challenges, algorithms offer a clear framework that guides computers through various operations, allowing for efficiency and precision in execution.

In the realm of computer science, the design and analysis of algorithms are crucial components that determine the performance and effectiveness of software applications. Students and tech founders alike need to understand the diverse types of algorithms available, from sorting and searching algorithms to more complex structures like graph and dynamic programming algorithms. Each category serves specific purposes and is optimized for particular types of problems, highlighting the importance of selecting the right algorithm based on the task at hand. This selection process is akin to how the human brain evaluates different strategies to arrive at a solution, often relying on experience and learned knowledge.

Moreover, algorithms are not just static sequences of instructions; they can evolve and adapt to new data, mimicking the plasticity of the human brain. Machine learning algorithms, for instance, learn from data inputs and improve their performance over time, much like how humans refine their skills through practice and feedback. This adaptive quality is central to artificial intelligence, enabling machines to perform tasks that require human-like reasoning and decision-making processes. Understanding this relationship between algorithms and adaptability can empower computer students and tech founders to create innovative solutions that push the boundaries of technology.

The implementation of algorithms also presents challenges that are reminiscent of cognitive difficulties humans face when solving problems. Issues such as computational complexity, efficiency, and scalability must be considered, as they directly influence the feasibility of solutions in real-world applications. Just as the human brain must manage cognitive load and prioritize information, computer scientists must optimize their algorithms to ensure that they can handle large datasets and complex operations without compromising performance. This intersection of human cognitive processes and algorithmic design underscores the importance of studying both fields in tandem.

In conclusion, algorithms play a pivotal role in problem-solving within the digital landscape, providing structured methodologies that mirror human cognitive strategies. For computer students and tech founders, a deep understanding of algorithms is essential not only for developing efficient software but also for fostering innovation in artificial intelligence and machine learning. By drawing inspiration from the human brain's problem-solving abilities, the next generation of technology leaders can create systems that not only mimic human thinking but also enhance it, leading to groundbreaking advancements in various domains.

Data Structures: Organizing Information

Data structures are essential components in computer science, serving as the foundation for organizing, storing, and managing information efficiently. In much the same way that the human brain categorizes and processes information, data structures enable computers to handle vast amounts of data systematically. By employing various data structures, computer programmers can optimize the performance of their applications, improving speed and efficiency in data retrieval and manipulation.

One of the most fundamental data structures is the array, which allows for the storage of a fixed-size sequence of elements. Arrays enable quick access to data through indexing, akin to how the brain retrieves memories based on location. However, they have limitations in terms of flexibility, as resizing an array requires creating a new one and copying data over. In contrast, linked lists offer a more dynamic approach to data organization, where each element, or node, points to the next. This structure facilitates easy insertions and deletions, mirroring the brain's ability to form and reform neural connections.

More complex data structures, such as trees and graphs, further enhance the capability of computers to manage hierarchical and relational data. Trees, for instance, mimic the branching patterns observed in the brain's neural networks, allowing for efficient searching and sorting through hierarchical relationships. Binary trees, a specific type of tree structure, enable logarithmic time complexity for search operations, making them invaluable in applications such as databases and file systems. Graphs, on the other hand, represent interconnected data points, similar to how the brain processes relationships and associations between different concepts, facilitating tasks such as social network analysis and route optimization.

Hash tables provide another powerful mechanism for organizing information, utilizing a technique that resembles the brain's associative memory function. By mapping keys to values through a hash function, hash tables allow for nearly instantaneous data retrieval. This efficiency is crucial in applications where speed is essential, such as caching and database indexing. However, developers must also consider the potential for hash collisions and how to manage them, paralleling the brain's ability to navigate similar or overlapping memories.

Understanding and selecting the appropriate data structure for a given task is vital for computer students and tech founders alike. The right choice can significantly impact the performance and scalability of an application, much like how an effective mental framework can enhance cognitive processing. As technology continues to evolve, the study of data structures will remain a cornerstone of computer science, reflecting the ongoing quest to develop systems that emulate human thought processes. By mastering these concepts, individuals in the tech industry can design more sophisticated algorithms and applications that align closely with the intricacies of human cognition.

CHAPTER 4

FROM BIOLOGY TO TECHNOLOGY: INSPIRATION FROM THE BRAIN

Biomimicry in Computing

Biomimicry in computing draws inspiration from the structures and processes found in nature, particularly the human brain, to enhance the design and functionality of computing systems. This approach leverages biological principles to solve complex computational problems, leading to innovations that mimic the efficiency and adaptability of natural systems. Understanding and applying these principles can offer computer students and tech founders a unique perspective on developing advanced technologies that operate with the sophistication of human cognitive functions.

One of the most significant examples of biomimicry in computing is the development of artificial neural networks, which are designed to replicate the way the human brain processes information. These networks consist of interconnected nodes that work together to recognize patterns, much like neurons in the brain. By mimicking the brain's ability to learn from experience, neural networks provide a powerful framework for machine learning applications, enabling computers to perform tasks such as image recognition, natural language processing, and decision-making with increasing accuracy.

Another area where biomimicry plays a crucial role is in the design of algorithms inspired by natural phenomena. For instance, swarm intelligence, which is derived from the collective behavior of social organisms like ants or bees, has led to the creation of algorithms that optimize problem-solving across various domains. These algorithms can efficiently navigate complex search spaces, making them useful for applications ranging from logistics to artificial intelligence. By studying how nature organizes and coordinates complex behaviors, computer scientists can develop more robust and scalable systems.

Moreover, the concept of evolutionary computing is another manifestation of biomimicry in computing. This approach emulates the process of natural selection to evolve solutions to optimization problems. By applying techniques such as genetic algorithms, computer systems can iteratively improve their performance by selecting the best solutions from a population, much like organisms adapt to their environments over generations. This method has proven effective in solving problems where traditional approaches may falter, highlighting the potential of nature-inspired strategies in advancing computational capabilities.

As the field of computing continues to evolve, the integration of biomimicry offers exciting opportunities for innovation. By fostering a deeper understanding of the human brain and other natural systems, computer students and tech founders can create technologies that not only enhance computational processes but also improve user interaction and experience. The future of computing may very well hinge on our ability to learn from nature, leading to systems that are not only powerful but also more intuitive and responsive to human needs.

Early Models of Artificial Intelligence

The early models of artificial intelligence (AI) laid the groundwork for the complex systems we see today. The inception of AI can be traced back to the mid-20th century when researchers began to explore the idea of machines simulating human intelligence. Pioneers like Alan Turing and John McCarthy sought to create models that could perform tasks typically requiring human cognition, such as problem-solving, understanding language, and recognizing patterns. Turing's concept of a "universal machine" and his famous Turing Test provided a theoretical framework for evaluating a machine's ability to exhibit intelligent behavior indistinguishable from that of a human.

One of the earliest forms of AI was symbolic AI, which relied on the manipulation of symbols to represent knowledge. This approach was based on the premise that human reasoning could be modeled through formal logic and rule-based systems. Early programs like the Logic Theorist and General Problem Solver exemplified this methodology by using heuristics to solve mathematical problems and perform logical reasoning. While these systems achieved impressive feats, they struggled with ambiguity and the vast complexity of real-world scenarios, limiting their practical applications.

Another significant development in early AI was the introduction of neural networks, inspired by the structure of the human brain. In the 1950s and 1960s, researchers like Frank Rosenblatt created the Perceptron, a simple model of a neuron that could learn to classify inputs. Although initially promising, these early neural networks faced challenges due to their inability to solve non-linear problems. It wasn't until the resurgence of interest in the 1980s, driven by advancements in computational power and the development of backpropagation algorithms, that neural networks began to realize their potential in mimicking complex cognitive functions.

Expert systems emerged in the late 1970s and 1980s as another early model of AI, focusing on specific domains of knowledge. These systems utilized a knowledge base and a set of rules to make inferences and solve problems within a particular area, such as medical diagnosis or financial forecasting. By encoding expert knowledge, systems like MYCIN and DENDRAL demonstrated the feasibility of using AI to replicate human expertise. However, their reliance on handcrafted rules limited scalability and adaptability, prompting researchers to explore more dynamic and flexible approaches.

As the field of AI evolved, the interplay between early models and advancements in computer science led to the development of more sophisticated algorithms and frameworks. The transition from rule-based systems to machine learning and deep learning marked a significant shift, allowing computers to learn from data and adapt to new situations. This progression reflects a deeper understanding of both human cognition and computational capabilities, paving the way for the powerful AI systems we rely on today. By studying these early models, computer students and tech founders can appreciate the foundational concepts that continue to influence modern AI research and applications.

Connectionism and Neural Networks

Connectionism is a theoretical framework in cognitive science that models mental or behavioral phenomena as the emergent processes of interconnected networks of simple units. It draws inspiration from the structure and functioning of the human brain, where neurons interconnect to process and transmit information. By simulating the way in which neurons work together to form complex cognitive functions, connectionism proposes that understanding human thought and behavior can be achieved through computational models that mirror these neural processes.

Neural networks, a key component of connectionism, are computational models designed to recognize patterns and make decisions based on input data. These networks consist of layers of interconnected nodes or "neurons," which process information by adjusting the strength of connections based on experience, akin to the way synapses are strengthened or weakened in biological brains. Each layer of a neural network transforms the data it receives, allowing for increasingly complex representations as information moves through the layers. This structure enables neural networks to perform tasks such as classification, regression, and even the generation of new data.

The learning process in neural networks is primarily achieved through a technique known as backpropagation, which involves adjusting the weights of connections based on errors in output. By iteratively refining these weights, the network improves its accuracy in predicting outcomes or recognizing patterns. This approach has been applied successfully in various applications, from image and speech recognition to natural language processing, thus demonstrating the versatility and power of neural networks in tackling complex problems that were previously beyond the reach of traditional programming methods.

Connectionism and neural networks also pose significant questions about the nature of intelligence and cognition. By demonstrating that networks can learn and adapt, they challenge traditional views of intelligence as a purely human trait. The capabilities of neural networks to achieve human-level performance in specific tasks raise philosophical and ethical considerations regarding the future of artificial intelligence. As these systems become more sophisticated, the potential for them to replicate aspects of human thought forces us to reconsider the boundaries between human cognition and machine processing.

In conclusion, the interplay between connectionism and neural networks not only enhances our understanding of how computers can mimic human thinking but also drives innovation in technology. For computer students and tech founders, exploring these concepts is crucial, as they form the foundation for developing advanced AI systems that can learn, adapt, and interact with the world in ways that were once thought exclusive to human intelligence. As the field continues to evolve, staying informed about the advancements in neural networks and their implications will be essential for those shaping the future of technology.

CHAPTER 5

MACHINE LEARNING: TEACHING COMPUTERS TO THINK

Types of Machine Learning

Machine learning, a subset of artificial intelligence, is a powerful tool that enables computers to learn from data and make decisions without explicit programming. It can be categorized into three main types: supervised learning, unsupervised learning, and reinforcement learning. Each type has its distinct methodologies and applications, catering to different needs in the field of computer science and technology. Understanding these types is crucial for computer students and tech founders as they explore the potential of machine learning in mimicking human cognitive processes.

Supervised learning involves training a model using a labeled dataset, where the inputs and corresponding outputs are known. The goal is to learn a mapping from inputs to outputs, allowing the model to predict outcomes for new, unseen data. Common applications include classification tasks, such as spam detection in emails, and regression tasks, like predicting housing prices. In supervised learning, the model is guided by the training data, similar to how a student learns from a teacher, making it an essential concept for those looking to develop predictive algorithms.

Unsupervised learning, on the other hand, deals with unlabeled data. The objective here is to discover hidden patterns or intrinsic structures within the data without predefined outputs. Techniques such as clustering and dimensionality reduction are prominent in this category. For instance, unsupervised learning can be used for customer segmentation in marketing, identifying distinct groups based on purchasing behavior. This type of learning mirrors certain aspects of human cognition, where individuals learn to identify patterns and make sense of new information without explicit guidance.

Reinforcement learning is another significant type of machine learning that focuses on training agents to make decisions through trial and error. In this framework, an agent interacts with an environment, receiving rewards or penalties based on its actions. The learning process is akin to how humans learn from experiences, adjusting their behaviors to maximize positive outcomes. Reinforcement learning has gained traction in various applications, including robotics, game playing, and autonomous systems, showing how machines can develop strategies akin to human decision-making.

In addition to these primary types, there are hybrid approaches that combine elements from different learning paradigms. For example, semi-supervised learning uses both labeled and unlabeled data to improve model performance, which is particularly useful when labeled data is scarce. Understanding these variations and their applications helps computer students and tech founders appreciate the nuances of machine learning and its relevance in building intelligent systems that emulate human-like reasoning and problem-solving abilities.

Supervised vs. Unsupervised Learning

Supervised learning and unsupervised learning are two primary paradigms in machine learning that reflect different approaches to data analysis and model training. In supervised learning, the algorithm is trained using a labeled dataset, meaning that each training example is paired with an output label. This approach allows the model to learn the relationship between input features and the corresponding output, enabling it to make predictions on new, unseen data. Common algorithms in this category include linear regression, decision trees, and support vector machines, which are widely used in tasks such as classification and regression.

In contrast, unsupervised learning deals with datasets that

do not have labeled outputs. The objective of unsupervised learning is to identify patterns or structures within the data without prior knowledge of the outcomes. This method is particularly useful in exploratory data analysis, clustering, and anomaly detection. Algorithms such as k-means clustering and hierarchical clustering fall under this category, allowing the system to group similar data points or identify outliers based on inherent characteristics, thereby revealing hidden relationships within the data.

The choice between supervised and unsupervised learning often depends on the nature of the problem and the available data. Supervised learning is typically employed when there is a clear target variable and ample labeled data, making it suitable for applications like spam detection or image recognition. On the other hand, unsupervised learning comes into play when the goal is to discover insights from data without predefined labels, such as segmenting customers in marketing or organizing large datasets for analysis. This flexibility allows machine learning practitioners to adapt their approaches based on the specific requirements of their projects.

Both supervised and unsupervised learning have their advantages and limitations. Supervised learning can achieve high accuracy in predictions when trained on high-quality labeled data; however, acquiring such data can be time-consuming and expensive. Conversely, unsupervised learning can process vast amounts of unlabeled data, making it a powerful tool for discovering new trends and insights. Nevertheless, it can be more challenging to evaluate the performance of unsupervised models, as there are no explicit metrics to measure their accuracy.

The intersection of supervised and unsupervised learning has led to the emergence of semi-supervised learning, which utilizes both labeled and unlabeled data to improve model performance. This hybrid approach leverages the strengths of both paradigms, allowing practitioners to build more robust models with less reliance on extensive labeled datasets. As machine learning continues to evolve, understanding these distinct methodologies and their applications will be essential for computer students and tech founders striving to develop innovative solutions that mimic human cognitive processes in the digital realm.

Deep Learning and Its Impact

Deep learning, a subset of artificial intelligence (AI), has revolutionized the way computers process and understand information, drawing inspiration from the neural networks that constitute the human brain. By mimicking the interconnected structure of neurons, deep learning algorithms can analyze vast amounts of data, identify patterns, and make predictions with remarkable accuracy. This technology has transformed a variety of fields, including image and speech recognition, natural language processing, and autonomous systems, showcasing its potential to enhance human capabilities and redefine our interactions with machines.

One of the most significant impacts of deep learning is its ability to improve the performance of tasks that were previously considered challenging for computers. For instance, deep learning models have surpassed traditional algorithms in image classification tasks, leading to advancements in fields such as healthcare, where they assist in diagnosing diseases from medical images. Similarly, in the realm of natural language processing, deep learning has enabled machines to understand and generate human language more effectively, resulting in sophisticated virtual assistants and translation services that are increasingly indistinguishable from human communication.

The proliferation of deep learning technologies has also sparked a surge in research and development within the tech industry. Startups and established companies alike are investing heavily in deep learning applications, seeking to harness its capabilities for innovative products and services. This has led to an ecosystem where collaboration between academia and industry is thriving, with researchers pushing the boundaries of what deep learning can achieve while practitioners apply these advancements to real-world problems. As a result, the landscape of technology is rapidly evolving, and those who understand deep learning's principles and applications are well-positioned to influence future developments.

Moreover, deep learning's impact extends beyond technical advancements; it raises important ethical and societal considerations. Issues such as bias in algorithms, data privacy, and the potential for job displacement due to automation have sparked discussions among technologists, policymakers, and the general public. As deep learning systems become more prevalent, it is crucial for computer students and tech founders to engage with these challenges, ensuring that the technology is developed and deployed responsibly. Addressing these concerns will be essential in building trust between users and AI systems, ultimately shaping the future of human-computer interaction.

In conclusion, deep learning has emerged as a transformative force in technology, mirroring the complexities of human cognition and enhancing our ability to process information. By understanding its principles and implications, computer students and tech founders can contribute to the responsible development of this technology, leveraging its potential while navigating the ethical challenges it presents. As we continue to explore the intersections between the human brain and computers, the ongoing evolution of deep learning promises to redefine not only how we interact with machines but also how we understand intelligence itself.

CHAPTER 6

NATURAL LANGUAGE PROCESSING: UNDERSTANDING HUMAN LANGUAGE

The Challenge of Language Interpretation

Language interpretation poses a significant challenge in the realm of artificial intelligence, particularly within natural language processing (NLP). Despite advancements in machine learning and computational linguistics, computers still struggle to grasp the nuances of human language. This difficulty arises from the inherent complexity of language, which includes idiomatic expressions, context-dependent meanings, and the subtleties of tone and emotion. These elements create a gap between human communicative intent and machine understanding, making it crucial for computer scientists and tech founders to focus on developing algorithms that can better interpret and emulate human-like comprehension.

One of the primary hurdles in language interpretation is ambiguity. Words and phrases can have multiple meanings depending on their context, leading to potential misinterpretations by machines. For instance, the word "bank" could refer to a financial institution or the side of a river. Humans naturally use contextual clues, intonation, and prior knowledge to deduce meaning, whereas computers rely on predefined algorithms that may not account for all variables. As a result, improving contextual awareness in machines is essential for enhancing their ability to interpret language accurately.

Another significant obstacle is the dynamic nature of language itself. Language evolves over time, with new slang, phrases, and grammatical structures emerging regularly. This fluidity can confound even the most sophisticated NLP systems, which often depend on static datasets for training. To address this, continuous learning mechanisms must be integrated into language processing technologies, allowing machines to adapt to linguistic changes and user-specific language patterns. Such adaptability is vital for applications ranging from virtual assistants to automated translation services.

Cultural differences further complicate language interpretation. Variations in dialects, idioms, and cultural references can lead to misunderstandings between machines and users from diverse backgrounds. For example, a phrase that is humorous in one culture may be offensive in another. Developing systems that can recognize and respect these cultural nuances is crucial for creating inclusive and effective communication tools. This requires not only advanced algorithms but also a deep understanding of sociolinguistics and cross-cultural communication.

Finally, the ethical implications of language interpretation cannot be overlooked. As machines become more capable of processing and generating human language, the potential for misuse increases. From generating misleading information to perpetuating biases present in training data, the consequences of flawed language interpretation can be severe. It is imperative for computer scientists and tech founders to prioritize ethical considerations in the development of NLP technologies, ensuring that their applications promote understanding rather than division. By addressing these challenges, the field can move closer to achieving a truly digital mind that reflects the complexity and richness of human thought.

Techniques in NLP

Natural Language Processing (NLP) encompasses a range of techniques that enable computers to understand, interpret, and respond to human language in a meaningful way. At its core, NLP combines the principles of linguistics and computer science, leveraging machine learning algorithms to analyze text and speech data. Among the foundational techniques are tokenization, which involves breaking down text into smaller units like words or phrases, and parsing, which focuses on analyzing grammatical structures. These techniques are essential for converting unstructured language data into a format that machines can process and understand.

Another crucial technique in NLP is named entity recognition (NER), which identifies and classifies key elements in text, such as names of people, organizations, locations, and dates. By extracting relevant entities, NER facilitates more nuanced understanding and context extraction from large datasets. This technique is particularly valuable in applications like search engines and information retrieval systems, where understanding the context behind user queries can significantly enhance the relevance of search results. Additionally, sentiment analysis is another important technique that assesses the emotional tone behind a body of text, allowing businesses to gauge customer opinions and reactions.

Machine learning models, particularly deep learning architectures like recurrent neural networks (RNNs) and transformers, have revolutionized NLP in recent years. These models are capable of capturing complex patterns and dependencies in language, enabling advancements in tasks such as language translation, summarization, and text generation. Transformers, in particular, with their attention mechanisms, allow models to weigh the importance of different words in a sentence, leading to more coherent and contextually appropriate outputs. This has opened up new possibilities for applications ranging from chatbots to automated content creation tools.

Pre-trained models, such as BERT (Bidirectional Encoder Representations from Transformers) and GPT (Generative Pre-trained Transformer), have further transformed the landscape of NLP. These models are trained on vast amounts of text data and can be fine-tuned for specific tasks, significantly reducing the time and resources required for developing high-performing NLP systems. The ability to leverage these pre-trained models has democratized access to advanced NLP capabilities, allowing smaller tech startups and individual developers to build sophisticated applications without extensive expertise in language processing.

Finally, ethical considerations in NLP techniques are becoming increasingly important. As algorithms are trained on data that may reflect biases present in society, the outcomes can inadvertently perpetuate stereotypes or misinformation. Addressing these challenges requires not only technical solutions, such as bias detection and mitigation strategies, but also a commitment to ethical AI practices. For computer students and tech founders, understanding these nuances is crucial for developing responsible NLP systems that align with societal values and contribute positively to the digital landscape.

Applications of NLP in Technology

Natural Language Processing (NLP) has emerged as a pivotal technology in the realm of artificial intelligence, significantly transforming how humans interact with machines. One of the most prominent applications of NLP is in virtual assistants, such as Siri, Alexa, and Google Assistant. These tools utilize NLP to understand user queries, process them, and deliver appropriate responses. By analyzing spoken or typed language, these virtual assistants can perform tasks ranging from setting reminders to controlling smart home devices. This seamless interaction exemplifies how NLP not only enhances user experience but also makes technology more accessible to a broader audience.

Another notable application of NLP is in sentiment analysis, which allows businesses to gauge consumer opinions and emotions through social media, reviews, and feedback. By employing NLP algorithms, companies can analyze large volumes of text data to identify trends and sentiments toward their products or services. This capability enables organizations to respond swiftly to customer needs and adapt their strategies accordingly. With the rise of social media and user-generated content, sentiment analysis has become a vital tool for businesses looking to maintain a competitive edge in the market.

NLP also plays a crucial role in content creation and curation. Automated systems can generate articles, summaries, and reports by analyzing existing data and extracting relevant information. For instance, news organizations utilize NLP algorithms to produce quick summaries of events, allowing readers to stay informed without wading through extensive articles. Furthermore, content recommendation systems leverage NLP to analyze user preferences and suggest articles, videos, or products that align with individual interests, enhancing user engagement and satisfaction.

In the field of education, NLP applications are revolutionizing the way students learn and interact with educational materials. Intelligent tutoring systems use NLP to provide personalized feedback and assistance, adapting to each learner's unique needs. These systems can analyze student responses in real-time, offering tailored recommendations and resources to facilitate deeper understanding. Additionally, language translation tools powered by NLP are breaking down language barriers, enabling students from diverse backgrounds to access educational content in their native languages.

Lastly, NLP contributes significantly to data analysis and information retrieval in various industries. Organizations employ NLP techniques to sift through vast datasets, extracting meaningful insights and patterns that would be challenging for humans to identify manually. This capability is particularly valuable in fields such as healthcare, where NLP can analyze clinical notes and research articles to uncover trends in patient care and treatment outcomes. By automating data processing and enhancing analytical capabilities, NLP empowers professionals to make informed decisions based on comprehensive insights, further bridging the gap between human cognition and machine intelligence.

CHAPTER 7

COGNITIVE COMPUTING: BEYOND TRADITIONAL AI

What is Cognitive Computing?

Cognitive computing refers to the simulation of human thought processes in a computerized model. This field combines elements from artificial intelligence, machine learning, and data analytics to create systems that can understand, reason, learn, and interact in a human-like manner. By mimicking human cognitive functions, these systems can process vast amounts of unstructured data, draw conclusions, and provide insights that can enhance decision-making in various applications, from healthcare to finance. The goal is to create machines that can not only perform tasks but also engage in conversations and understand context, making them more intuitive and user-friendly.

At the core of cognitive computing is the ability to learn from experiences. Unlike traditional computing systems that rely on programmed responses, cognitive systems utilize algorithms that enable them to adapt and improve over time. These systems utilize techniques such as natural language processing (NLP), which allows them to comprehend and generate human language, and machine learning, which enables them to identify patterns and make predictions based on historical data. As cognitive systems are exposed to more data, they refine their abilities, much like the human brain develops through learning and experience.

One significant aspect of cognitive computing is its application in real-world scenarios. In healthcare, for example, cognitive systems can analyze patient data to suggest personalized treatment plans, predict patient outcomes, and assist doctors in diagnosing diseases more accurately. In the financial sector, cognitive computing can detect fraudulent transactions by learning to recognize anomalies in spending patterns. These applications highlight the potential of cognitive systems to augment human capabilities and improve efficiency across various industries, reflecting a shift toward more intelligent and adaptable technology.

The intersection of cognitive computing and neuroscience is particularly profound. Understanding how the human brain processes information has inspired the development of cognitive systems. Researchers study brain functions, such as memory, attention, and decision-making, to inform the design of algorithms that mimic these processes. This collaboration between fields not only advances technology but also enriches our understanding of human cognition, paving the way for innovations that could ultimately bridge the gap between human and machine intelligence.

As cognitive computing continues to evolve, it raises important questions about the future of human-computer interaction. The potential for machines to understand and respond to human emotions, preferences, and behaviors suggests a future where technology is seamlessly integrated into daily life. For computer students and tech founders, this presents both opportunities and challenges, as they must navigate the ethical implications and societal impacts of creating machines that think and learn like humans. The development of cognitive computing systems is not just a technological endeavor; it is a journey toward understanding what it means to think, learn, and interact in a digital age.

Key Technologies and Frameworks

The exploration of key technologies and frameworks that facilitate the mimicry of human thinking by computers is essential for understanding the intersection of artificial intelligence and neuroscience. Central to this discussion is the concept of neural networks, which are computational models inspired by the human brain's structure and function. These networks consist of interconnected nodes or neurons that process information in a manner similar to biological neurons. By employing layers of these nodes, neural networks can learn to identify patterns, classify data, and make predictions, thereby enabling machines to perform tasks that were once thought to require human intelligence.

Deep learning, a subset of machine learning, is another crucial technology in this arena. It employs multiple layers of neural networks to analyze vast amounts of data. This technique has led to significant advancements in various fields, such as image and speech recognition, natural language processing, and autonomous systems. The ability of deep learning models to automatically extract features from raw data has revolutionized how computers can interpret complex information, positioning them closer to human-like understanding. Frameworks like TensorFlow and PyTorch have emerged as powerful tools for developers, allowing for the efficient design, training, and deployment of deep learning models.

Natural language processing (NLP) is another area where technology strives to replicate human cognitive abilities. NLP techniques enable computers to understand, interpret, and generate human language, bridging the gap between human communication and machine comprehension. Through models like BERT and GPT, NLP has made significant strides in understanding context, sentiment, and nuanced language. These advancements are crucial for applications ranging from chatbots to advanced translation services, as they allow machines to engage in more human-like conversations and interactions.

Reinforcement learning (RL) represents another key framework that draws on principles of human learning and decision-making. In RL, agents learn to make decisions by receiving feedback from their environment, similar to how humans learn from experiences. This method has been effectively employed in various applications, including robotics, gaming, and even financial modeling. By simulating environments and allowing agents to explore different strategies, RL provides insights into optimizing behavior and achieving complex goals, mirroring the human capacity for learning through trial and error.

Finally, the integration of these technologies and frameworks is often facilitated by software tools and platforms designed to support AI development. Tools such as Jupyter Notebooks enable experimentation and visualization, while cloud-based services provide the necessary computational power to handle intensive processing tasks. These resources make it easier for computer students and tech founders to experiment with and implement sophisticated algorithms, fostering innovation and the advancement of intelligent systems. As these technologies continue to evolve, they promise to unlock new possibilities for creating machines that not only mimic but also enhance human cognitive capabilities.

Real-World Applications and Case Studies

Real-world applications of digital mimicking of human thinking have continued to evolve, demonstrating the potential of computers to enhance various sectors. One prominent case is in healthcare, where machine learning algorithms are employed to analyze medical data, predict disease outbreaks, and assist in diagnostics. For instance, IBM's Watson Health utilizes artificial intelligence to sift through vast amounts of medical literature and patient records, providing physicians with evidence-based treatment options. This capability not only supports doctors in making informed decisions but also accelerates the research process, showcasing how computer systems can replicate cognitive tasks traditionally performed by humans.

In the realm of finance, algorithms that replicate human decision-making processes have transformed trading practices. High-frequency trading firms leverage AI to analyze market trends and execute trades at speeds unattainable by human traders. An example of this is the use of natural language processing to evaluate news articles and social media sentiment, allowing algorithms to predict stock movements based on public perception. This application not only improves trading efficiency but also highlights the ability of computers to mimic nuanced human cognitive functions like interpretation and judgment.

The education sector has also embraced digital tools that emulate human thinking patterns. Adaptive learning technologies, such as those developed by Knewton, analyze student performance in real-time and tailor educational content to meet individual learning needs. By employing algorithms that recognize patterns in student behavior, these systems can provide personalized feedback and resources, enhancing the learning experience. The integration of such technologies demonstrates how digital systems can mimic the adaptive and responsive qualities of human educators, ultimately fostering better learning outcomes.

Moreover, in the field of customer service, chatbots and virtual assistants have become indispensable tools for businesses. Companies like Zendesk and Drift utilize AI-driven chatbots that can engage in meaningful conversations with customers, answering queries and resolving issues with minimal human intervention. By using machine learning to understand context and intention, these systems can provide responses that closely resemble human interaction. This advancement not only improves customer satisfaction but also allows businesses to allocate human resources more effectively, demonstrating the practical benefits of computer systems that mimic human thought processes.

Lastly, the transportation industry has seen significant advancements through the adoption of AI technologies that simulate human decision-making. Autonomous vehicles, such as those developed by Tesla and Waymo, rely on complex algorithms that replicate the cognitive functions involved in driving. These vehicles analyze their surroundings, make split-second decisions, and learn from vast datasets of driving scenarios. The successful implementation of these systems illustrates the potential for computers to not only replicate human thinking but also enhance safety and efficiency in transportation, signaling a future where AI and human-like reasoning are integral to everyday life.

CHAPTER 8

ETHICAL CONSIDERATIONS IN MIMICKING HUMAN THOUGHT

The Ethics of Artificial Intelligence

The ethics of artificial intelligence (AI) is a critical topic that intersects with the development and deployment of technology in ways that affect society at large. As computer students and tech founders navigate the complexities of AI, understanding the ethical implications becomes paramount. The rapid advancement of AI technologies raises questions about accountability, transparency, and the potential for bias in algorithms. These concerns are not merely academic; they impact real-world applications in areas such as healthcare, finance, and law enforcement. As AI systems become increasingly autonomous, the stakes regarding ethical considerations grow higher.

One of the most pressing ethical issues in AI is the potential for bias in decision-making processes. Algorithms trained on historical data can inadvertently perpetuate existing biases present in that data, leading to discriminatory outcomes. For instance, if an AI system is used in hiring practices and is trained on data that reflects historical gender or racial disparities, it may reinforce those inequalities. Computer students and tech founders must be aware of these pitfalls and actively work to ensure that their AI systems are designed to mitigate bias. This involves employing diverse datasets, implementing fairness criteria, and conducting regular audits to assess the impact of AI decisions on different demographic groups.

Transparency in AI is another vital ethical concern. As AI systems become more complex, understanding how they arrive at specific decisions becomes challenging. This "black box" phenomenon can erode trust in AI technologies, especially when users are affected by the outcomes of these systems without a clear understanding of the underlying processes. For tech founders, fostering transparency involves creating explainable AI models that allow users to comprehend how decisions are made. This not only enhances user trust but also encourages responsible use of AI technologies, as stakeholders can better assess the implications of automated decisions.

Accountability in AI development is also essential. As AI systems are deployed in critical areas such as autonomous vehicles or healthcare diagnostics, the question of who is responsible for errors or harms caused by these technologies becomes increasingly complex. Computer students and tech founders should consider the implications of liability in their designs and seek to establish frameworks that ensure accountability. This might include implementing rigorous testing protocols, maintaining documentation of decision-making processes, and establishing clear lines of responsibility among developers, organizations, and users.

Finally, the ethical considerations surrounding AI extend beyond immediate technological concerns to broader societal implications. As AI continues to evolve, it raises questions about privacy, surveillance, and the potential for job displacement. The balance between innovation and ethical responsibility is delicate, requiring ongoing dialogue among computer scientists, policymakers, and ethicists. For tech founders, engaging with these discussions and incorporating ethical considerations into the design and deployment of AI systems is not only a moral imperative but also a strategic necessity in fostering sustainable and socially responsible technology.

Implications for Society and Employment

The interplay between digital technology and human cognition has profound implications for society and employment. As computers increasingly mimic human thinking, their integration into various sectors alters the nature of work and the skills required from the workforce. This transformation challenges traditional employment models, necessitating new approaches to education and training. The shift towards automation and artificial intelligence raises questions about job displacement, workforce adaptability, and the economic landscape.

One significant implication is the potential for job displacement in sectors heavily reliant on routine tasks. As machines become capable of performing cognitive tasks traditionally reserved for humans, such as data analysis and decision-making, many roles may become obsolete. This phenomenon is already observable in industries like manufacturing and customer service, where automation streamlines operations and reduces labor costs. Consequently, workers in these sectors must adapt by acquiring skills that complement the capabilities of digital technologies, rather than compete against them.

Moreover, the demand for new skill sets is reshaping educational priorities. Computer students and tech founders must recognize the importance of interdisciplinary knowledge that blends technical expertise with soft skills such as critical thinking, creativity, and emotional intelligence. As the workforce evolves, educational institutions are tasked with preparing students for a landscape where adaptability and continuous learning become paramount. Curriculums that emphasize collaboration and problem-solving will equip future professionals to thrive in a digital economy.

The rise of digital technologies also fosters the emergence of new job categories and industries. Roles in artificial intelligence, machine learning, and data science are gaining prominence, reflecting the need for specialized knowledge in these areas. Additionally, as businesses leverage technology for innovation, entrepreneurial opportunities abound. Tech founders can capitalize on the convergence of human cognition and computing by developing solutions that address societal challenges, thereby driving economic growth and job creation.

Finally, the societal implications of this technological evolution extend beyond employment to encompass ethical considerations. As computers increasingly mimic human decision-making, issues of bias, accountability, and privacy come to the forefront. Society must grapple with the ethical ramifications of relying on algorithms to make critical decisions, such as in healthcare and criminal justice. Engaging in discussions about the responsible development and deployment of technology is essential for ensuring that the benefits of digital advancements are equitably distributed and do not perpetuate existing inequalities.

Addressing Bias in Algorithms

Addressing bias in algorithms is a critical concern in the intersection of artificial intelligence and human cognition. Algorithms, which are designed to process data and make decisions, often inadvertently reflect the biases present in the datasets they are trained on. These biases can stem from various sources, including societal norms, historical prejudices, and the subjective choices made during data collection and processing. For computer students and tech founders, understanding how these biases manifest and affect algorithmic outcomes is essential for developing ethical and effective technology.

The first step in addressing bias involves recognizing its sources. Data used for training algorithms can be skewed in various ways, such as through underrepresentation of certain groups or overrepresentation of others. For instance, facial recognition software has been shown to perform more accurately on lighter-skinned individuals compared to those with darker skin tones. This discrepancy can lead to real-world consequences, such as misidentification or exclusion from services. By examining the origins of the data and ensuring diverse representation, developers can create more equitable algorithms.

Once biases are identified, it is crucial to implement strategies for mitigation. One effective method is to employ fairness-aware algorithms that actively seek to minimize bias in their outputs. This can involve techniques such as re-weighting training data or employing adversarial training methods that penalize biased predictions. Additionally, fostering collaboration between technologists and social scientists can provide valuable insights into the societal implications of algorithms, allowing for a more holistic approach to bias reduction.

Transparency and accountability are also vital components in the fight against algorithmic bias. Developers should strive to make their algorithms interpretable, allowing users to understand how decisions are made. This transparency can help identify underlying biases and prompt necessary adjustments. Furthermore, establishing frameworks for accountability, where organizations are responsible for their algorithmic decisions, can encourage a culture of ethical responsibility in tech development.

Lastly, continuous monitoring and evaluation of algorithms are necessary to ensure that biases do not resurface over time. As societal norms evolve, so too should the algorithms that influence various aspects of life. By implementing regular audits and updates, tech founders can ensure that their systems remain fair and relevant. This proactive approach not only enhances the integrity of technology but also promotes trust among users, affirming the commitment to developing tools that truly enhance human decision-making.

CHAPTER 9

FUTURE TRENDS IN DIGITAL MINDS

Advancements in AI and Cognitive Technologies

Advancements in artificial intelligence (AI) and cognitive technologies have transformed the way we understand and replicate human thinking processes. Over the past few decades, significant strides have been made in machine learning, natural language processing, and neural networks, which have allowed computers to tackle complex tasks that were once the domain of human intelligence. These technologies have evolved from basic algorithms to sophisticated systems capable of learning from experience, making decisions, and even exhibiting creativity. As computer students and tech founders delve into this field, it becomes crucial to grasp the foundational concepts and the implications of these advancements on both technology and society.

One of the most notable advancements in AI is the development of deep learning, a subset of machine learning that utilizes neural networks with numerous layers. This approach has led to breakthroughs in image and speech recognition, enabling machines to interpret and respond to visual and auditory data with remarkable accuracy. For instance, deep learning algorithms have been instrumental in enhancing the capabilities of virtual assistants, such as Siri and Alexa, allowing them to understand and process natural language more effectively. Understanding these mechanisms offers insights into how computers can mimic human cognitive functions, paving the way for innovations in various applications, from healthcare to autonomous vehicles.

Cognitive technologies have also made significant headway in the realm of data analysis and decision-making. With the ability to process vast amounts of information at unprecedented speeds,

AI systems can uncover patterns and insights that would be impossible for humans to discern. These capabilities are not just limited to straightforward data processing; they extend to predictive analytics, where AI can forecast trends and behaviors based on historical data. This has profound implications for businesses and industries, as tech founders can leverage these technologies to enhance operational efficiency, optimize resource allocation, and drive strategic decision-making.

Furthermore, the integration of AI with other emerging technologies, such as the Internet of Things (IoT) and blockchain, has opened new frontiers for cognitive computing. The convergence of these technologies allows for the creation of intelligent systems that can learn and adapt in real-time, enhancing their ability to respond to dynamic environments. For example, smart home devices equipped with AI can learn user preferences and automate processes to improve convenience and energy efficiency. As students and entrepreneurs explore these intersections, they can identify opportunities to innovate and develop solutions that address pressing challenges in various sectors.

Ethical considerations surrounding AI and cognitive technologies also warrant attention. As these systems become more prevalent, issues such as data privacy, algorithmic bias, and the potential for job displacement arise. It is essential for future tech leaders to engage with these ethical dilemmas and prioritize responsible AI development. By fostering an understanding of the ethical implications of their work, computer students and tech founders can contribute to a future where AI enhances human capabilities while safeguarding societal values. Embracing advancements in AI and cognitive technologies requires not only technical proficiency but also a commitment to ethical responsibility and sustainable innovation.

The Role of Quantum Computing

Quantum computing represents a significant paradigm shift in computational capabilities, poised to revolutionize the way we approach complex problems. Unlike classical computers, which process information in bits, quantum computers utilize qubits that can exist in multiple states simultaneously. This property, known as superposition, allows quantum computers to perform calculations at unprecedented speeds, making them ideal for tasks that involve vast amounts of data or intricate problem-solving. As computer students and tech founders delve into the intersection of human cognition and computational power, understanding the implications of quantum computing becomes essential.

One of the most compelling applications of quantum computing lies in its potential to enhance artificial intelligence. Traditional machine learning algorithms often struggle with large datasets or require extensive time to identify patterns. Quantum algorithms, however, can analyze these datasets more efficiently by leveraging quantum phenomena such as entanglement and superposition. This capability not only accelerates machine learning processes but also enables the development of more sophisticated AI systems that can mimic human cognitive functions more closely. As a result, tech founders are increasingly exploring quantum computing to create innovative AI solutions that can outperform classical counterparts.

Moreover, quantum computing holds promise for solving problems that are currently intractable for classical machines. For example, optimization problems prevalent in logistics, finance, and pharmaceuticals often involve numerous variables and potential solutions. Quantum algorithms can evaluate multiple possibilities simultaneously, leading to faster and more accurate results. This ability to tackle complex optimization challenges could significantly impact various industries, driving advancements in resource allocation, supply chain management, and drug discovery. Understanding these applications is crucial for computer students as they prepare to enter a workforce that increasingly values quantum computing expertise.

The intersection of quantum computing and cryptography also warrants attention, as it poses both opportunities and challenges. Quantum computers could potentially break widely used encryption protocols, jeopardizing data security across the digital landscape. However, they also pave the way for quantum encryption methods, which leverage the principles of quantum mechanics to create unbreakable codes. For tech founders, this duality highlights the importance of developing secure systems that can withstand the capabilities of quantum machines. As such, a thorough comprehension of quantum cryptography is becoming an essential part of modern cybersecurity strategies.

As we continue to explore the role of quantum computing, it is imperative to consider its ethical implications and societal impact. The powerful capabilities of quantum computers raise questions about accessibility, equity, and the potential for misuse. As computer students and tech founders engage with this technology, they must remain vigilant about the ethical dimensions of their work. Responsible innovation will be key in ensuring that the benefits of quantum computing are harnessed for the greater good while minimizing risks associated with its deployment in society. In this evolving landscape, a collaborative approach among technologists, ethicists, and policymakers will be essential to navigate the complexities of quantum computing and its integration into our digital lives.

Predictions for the Next Decade

As we look to the next decade, the intersection of human cognition and digital technology is poised to evolve in unprecedented ways. Advances in artificial intelligence and machine learning will increasingly allow computers to not just mimic human thought but to enhance and expand upon it. We can anticipate significant improvements in natural language processing, enabling machines to understand and generate human-like language with remarkable accuracy. This will facilitate deeper interactions between humans and machines, fostering environments where technology can assist in creative processes, education, and even emotional support.

Another area ripe for development is the integration of neuroscience and computer science. As researchers gain a better understanding of the human brain's workings, we can expect to see more sophisticated algorithms that are inspired by neural processes. These algorithms will not only be more efficient but will also be capable of learning from fewer data points, much like humans do. This shift could lead to breakthroughs in personalized computing, where systems adapt to individual user preferences and behaviors, thus creating tailored experiences that enhance productivity and satisfaction.

Moreover, the ethical implications of these advancements will become increasingly critical. As technology begins to replicate human decision-making processes, questions surrounding accountability, bias, and transparency will need to be addressed. The next decade will likely see the emergence of new frameworks and regulations aimed at governing the use of AI in sensitive areas such as healthcare, law enforcement, and education. Tech founders and computer students must engage with these ethical challenges, ensuring that the systems they develop prioritize human welfare and societal benefit.

The role of human cognition in the development of intelligent systems will also shift. As computers become more adept at solving complex problems, the emphasis will likely move towards augmenting human skills rather than replacing them. This collaboration between human intuition and machine computation could lead to hybrid decision-making models, where the strengths of both parties are leveraged to achieve outcomes that neither could accomplish alone. Educational frameworks will need to adapt, preparing future computer scientists to work alongside intelligent systems by fostering skills that emphasize critical thinking and creativity.

Finally, we can expect the digital landscape to reshape the way we perceive and interact with our own minds. As technology continues to evolve, it will influence our cognitive processes, potentially changing the way we think, learn, and remember. The next decade may witness the rise of brain-computer interfaces that blur the lines between human thought and digital processing, leading to new forms of communication and expression. Computer students and tech founders will play a crucial role in exploring these frontiers, driving innovations that not only mimic but also enhance the capabilities of the human mind.

CHAPTER 10

CONCLUSION: BRIDGING THE GAP BETWEEN HUMANS AND MACHINES

Summary of Key Insights

The exploration of how computers mimic human thinking reveals several key insights that are essential for both computer students and tech founders. One of the most significant takeaways is the profound relationship between neural networks and the human brain. Neural networks, inspired by the structure and function of human neurons, have transformed the landscape of artificial intelligence. Understanding this relationship can empower students and founders to create more sophisticated algorithms that approximate human cognitive processes, leading to advancements in fields such as machine learning and artificial intelligence.

Another critical insight is the importance of data in training computational models. Just as human learning is heavily dependent on experience, the efficacy of computer systems hinges on the quality and quantity of data they are exposed to. This highlights a crucial aspect for tech founders: the necessity of implementing robust data collection and management strategies. By ensuring high-quality input, founders can enhance the performance of their technologies, making them more adept at tasks that require human-like reasoning and decision-making.

Furthermore, the concept of adaptability emerges as a key insight in the digital mind framework. Human beings are remarkable in their ability to learn from changing environments and adjust their behavior accordingly. Similarly, the development of adaptive algorithms that can improve over time through reinforcement learning is vital for building systems that thrive in dynamic conditions. Computer students should focus on the principles of adaptability, as this will prepare them for future challenges in creating intelligent systems that can operate effectively in unpredictable real-world scenarios.

The ethical implications of mimicking human thought processes also stand out as an essential consideration. As computers increasingly take on roles that require cognitive functions, ethical dilemmas arise regarding privacy, autonomy, and decision-making. For tech founders, recognizing the responsibility that comes with creating such technologies is imperative. They must prioritize ethical frameworks in their development processes to ensure that their innovations benefit society without compromising individual rights or freedoms.

Finally, interdisciplinary collaboration emerges as a vital insight for fostering innovation in the realm of computer science and cognitive studies. Engaging with experts from psychology, neuroscience, and philosophy can provide a more holistic understanding of human cognition and its application to technology. For both computer students and tech founders, cultivating a collaborative mindset can lead to groundbreaking discoveries and advancements that bridge the gap between human intelligence and computational capabilities, ultimately driving the future of technology forward.

The Future of Human-Computer Interaction

The future of human-computer interaction (HCI) is poised for revolutionary changes, driven by advancements in artificial intelligence, machine learning, and natural language processing. As computers become increasingly capable of understanding and processing human behavior and emotions, the ways in which people interact with technology will evolve significantly. This shift is not merely a matter of improving user interfaces but rather a fundamental transformation in how we conceive of and engage with digital systems. The integration of AI into HCI will enable more intuitive interactions that mimic human cognitive processes, thereby enhancing the overall user experience.

One of the most promising developments is the rise of

conversational interfaces, including chatbots and voice-activated assistants. These tools allow users to communicate with computers in a more natural and fluid manner, resembling human dialogue. As natural language processing continues to improve, these interfaces will become more adept at understanding context, tone, and intent. This capability has the potential to reshape various industries, from customer service to education, by providing personalized support and information tailored to individual needs. For computer students and tech founders, harnessing these technologies will be crucial for developing applications that resonate with users on a deeper level.

Moreover, the incorporation of augmented reality (AR) and virtual reality (VR) into HCI will further enhance the way individuals interact with digital environments. These immersive technologies allow users to engage with digital content in a spatial context, bridging the gap between the physical and digital worlds. For instance, in fields such as architecture and design, AR and VR can facilitate collaborative projects by allowing teams to visualize and manipulate digital models in real time. As HCI evolves to include these immersive experiences, the demand for skilled professionals who can create and manage such technologies will increase, presenting exciting opportunities for innovation.

Another critical aspect of the future of HCI is the emphasis on accessibility and inclusivity. As technology becomes more integrated into daily life, ensuring that all individuals, regardless of ability, can interact with digital systems is paramount. Future developments in HCI will likely prioritize adaptive technologies that respond to the unique needs of users, such as customizable interfaces for individuals with disabilities. This focus will not only broaden the user base for many applications but also push tech founders to consider ethical implications and the societal impact of their innovations.

Ultimately, the future of human-computer interaction will be characterized by a deeper understanding of human cognition and behavior. As machines become more capable of mimicking these processes, the synergy between humans and computers will foster new forms of collaboration and creativity. For computer students and tech founders, staying ahead of these trends and understanding the underlying principles of HCI will be essential for developing technologies that not only meet users' needs but also enhance their capabilities. By embracing this evolving landscape, the next generation of innovators can create solutions that truly reflect the intricacies of the human mind and its interaction with the digital realm.

Final Thoughts and Call to Action

As we reach the conclusion of our exploration into how computers mimic human thinking, it is vital to reflect on the profound implications of this intersection between technology and human cognition. The advancements in artificial intelligence and machine learning showcase not only the capabilities of computers but also the potential to enhance our understanding of the human brain. By studying these systems, we gain insights into cognitive processes, decision-making, and even emotional responses, fostering a deeper appreciation for the complexities of human intelligence.

The relationship between the human brain and computers poses intriguing questions about identity, creativity, and the future of work. As technology continues to evolve, the lines between human and machine intelligence blur. This convergence invites computer students and tech founders to consider the ethical ramifications of their creations. The responsibility to harness technology for the betterment of society is paramount, ensuring that advancements serve humanity rather than detract from it. As future leaders in the tech industry, you must be vigilant about the societal implications of the technologies you develop.

Furthermore, the rapid pace of innovation in computing

offers a unique opportunity for collaboration across disciplines. Computer students should seek to engage with fields such as neuroscience, psychology, and ethics to enhance their understanding of human cognition. This interdisciplinary approach will not only equip you with a broader perspective but also inspire novel solutions to complex problems. By fostering a culture of collaboration, we can drive advancements that respect and reflect the intricacies of human thought.

As we look ahead, it becomes clear that the future of technology is not solely about creating smarter machines but also about augmenting human capabilities. Tech founders must prioritize developing tools that empower individuals rather than replace them. This commitment can lead to innovations that enhance creativity, improve mental health, and facilitate meaningful human connections. The challenge lies in balancing technological progress with the preservation of what makes us distinctly human.

In closing, I urge you to embrace the responsibility that comes with the power of technology. As computer students and tech founders, your roles will shape the future landscape of human-computer interaction. Stay curious, engage with diverse perspectives, and remain committed to ethical practices. By doing so, you will not only contribute to the advancement of technology but also ensure that it serves as a bridge between human potential and digital innovation. The journey ahead is filled with promise, and your actions can make a significant difference in how this narrative unfolds.

ABOUT THE AUTHOR

Golf Ofuka

Golf Ofuka is the dynamic CEO and Founder of gcodecloud GmbH and Mega Phonebook Nig, recognized for his innovative approach to technology and business. His career and entrepreneurial journey highlight his expertise in the software and IT industry, alongside a robust knowledge of business strategy, development, and market positioning. Based in Berlin, Germany, Golf leverages his strong technical foundation and a sharp business acumen to spearhead ventures that bridge technological innovation with market needs.

Background and Leadership
Golf's career path reflects a blend of technology mastery and entrepreneurial insight, making him a valuable leader in today's fast-paced digital landscape. As the CEO and driving force behind gcodecloud GmbH, he leads a team that is transforming software solutions for modern enterprises. His leadership is marked by a deep commitment to fostering innovation within his organization and a clear vision for scaling products and services that meet the evolving demands of global markets.

Similarly, through his leadership at Mega Phonebook Nig, Golf demonstrates his commitment to impactful solutions by connecting businesses and individuals across various communication and data management platforms. His approach emphasizes usability and accessibility, making it easier for clients to integrate these solutions seamlessly into their operations.

www.ingramcontent.com/pod-product-compliance
Lightning Source LLC
Chambersburg PA
CBHW070402230526
45471CB00006B/2666